Table of Contents

INTRODUCTION

Keep Investing, People often say the first million is the hardest million. That is especially true when investing. If you reach retirement with a large investment nest egg, you could increase your wealth by remaining aggressive with your investments. For instance, if you have $1 million in investable assets when you reach retirement along with a pension and Social Security, you could double your investment over a 20 year period if you average 4% per year. This means it is possible to make some withdrawals from your portfolio and still double your wealth if the sequence of your returns works in your favor, but who wants to become a millionaire by age 65?

For retirees facing a savings shortfall or for those that just want to increase their wealth, there are a number of options available to do so, but there isn't any easy way to make millions. Retirement planning can be hard, especially when you want to continue to increase your wealth at a time when so many people are struggling to get by from year to year.

For those with high earning jobs, consulting opportunities, or a large investment account in retirement, there are more options to make money in retirement. For You, cutting expenses, continuing to work, and deferring Social Security can all add up to big bucks over time.

This book explain more better on the F.I.R.E Movement, Financial Independence and Retiring early. The most efficient, proven & fastest ways to your early retirement.

FINANCIAL INDEPENDENCE

Financial independence: it is the ultimate frugal goal, but what does it mean really? There are three definitions for financial independence. They are:

1 Not relying on others to pay your bills

2 Freedom from all debt

3 Freedom from having to work for income

I tend to regard financial independence as a

combination of the three; and so, for me, financial independence is not something that is easily gained. I don't rely on others to pay my bills, but I'm still socking away money to reach a point where I don't have to work to live. Where are you at in your quest for financial freedom? What have done to get there?

At times dealing with bills, earnings, expenses and other aspects of money create challenges for many people. Some people struggle to get by, in fact, there are so many who would have been super-successful but for their inability to handle and tame money cost them but, I tell you, you can master money. If you do not know how to make, manage and multiply money with peace of mind, you cannot claim to be successful in life if you are not financially successful because you need money to fuel your other goals in life, be it marital success, business success, health success or academic success.

You must know these points.

Without financial independence, you are a slave to money.

Achieving financial independence will take time, dedication and lots of hard work but will be worth it in the end.

Remember, money is not everything. It has been said that money is the root of all evil, but only an obsession and love of money for its own sake, I believe is bad.

Nearly everyone has the ability to be successful, but very few have the desire as well as the commitment to make the sacrifices necessary to achieve wealth. We believe the goal is beyond reach & impossible thus, giving up before even starting.

Whether you are struggling or just want to maximize your wealth, there are several things you can do to improve your financial outlook.

When it comes to financial independence, it often seems that there are certain members of society who just have a better chance of succeeding than everyone else. In fact, there is a anecdote that makes the rounds every so often that claims if you take a group of millionaires; remove all of their knowledge, wealth, and experience; and stick them in the middle of a desert with nothing but a gallon of water, almost every single one of them will be back to millionaire status within 10 years. While it is hardly ethical or scientific to actually put this theory to a test, the basic premise is pretty reasonable: the wealthy are wealthy because finances, investments, and making money are what they're good at doing.

Moreover, researches have shown that over 70% of millionaires were self made, and 78% were from the middle class or poor. So we don't have to argue about the 'wealthy parents' part.

Your Goals, Your Life

While it may not be your life goal to become a millionaire, it would be difficult to convince anyone that being financially independent or comfortably wealthy wouldn't be a nice break from the routine of everyday life. Yet few people really take advantage of what they currently have to try and amass the kind of wealth that will allow them an early retirement or that beach house in the Grand Caymans.

This may seem oversimplified at first, but the fact is, most people view financial investments or long-term financial planning as something that can wait or that can be set aside when everyday life gets in the way.

The best financial advisors and investment firms, however, will tell you that the first thing you can do to start making the kinds of decisions that will create a solid portfolio of wealth for the future is to sit down and really outline what it is you want and what steps you can take to get there.

For example, imagine a family whose three children are only a year apart in age. They're young right now, but the parents one day hope to see all of them in the college of their dreams. There are a number of steps that necd be taken to make that goal a reality, and not all of them have to do with stepping up the piano lessons or moving to a neighborhood with the best public schools. In order to reasonably put three kids through college, it is best to create a financial plan with actual, numerical results at the end. Saving whatever is left at the end of the month is a good first step, but unless you sit down and look at what kinds of investments that money needs to go into to get the necessary percentage increase in 15 years, you aren't following a financial plan - you're just saving money.

Understanding that difference - the difference between saving money and following a financial plan - is what really separates the millionaires from the rest of the population.

The good news is, in today's world, you don't have to have the know-how yourself to move from saving to creating an investment plan. Thanks to financial advisors and other professional firms dedicated to turning fiscal dreams into realities.

But I am here to tell you, that creating your own financial & retirement plan is a thousand times better than consulting a financial advisor IF you do your due diligence & research correctly, as most financial advisors will take a hefty percentage of managing your portfolio which is going to snowball to huge amounts over time.

Tips to Financial Independence

These are the 7 secrets to financial independence, read them, take them in and execute them.

TAKE ACTION NOW!

If you don't take the action necessary to achieve financial independence and success, to improve your life, you will no doubt wind up right alongside the 95 percent of the population that is dependent on debt and are ultimately financial failures.

If you think you are starting late, then worry no further because starting now is the earliest you can start.

2 - The level of success you achieve in your life is directly proportional to your willingness to accept full responsibility for your life.

These are not the early times where saving 10% or 20% of your monthly salary is enough.

Save atleast 50%, live like a beggar when you are young to retire as an early millionaire in your 30's.

No matter where you are now, you can only achieve greater things if you take blame and hold yourself accountable for your past. Accept your past and grasp hold of your future.

3 - Failing to execute a plan for financial independence is the same as planning to fail.

This seems fairly self evident. People just float around through their financial life hoping it will all somehow just work out. This is not only wrong but it reeks of insanity.

You can't just approximate your spendings, savings & goals. Plan them, Write them down to the nearest cent and become obsessed with them.

Start right now like your hair is on fire and do whatever it costs to stay on track. The faster you achieve the plan, the longer you can enjoy mojitos in Hawaii. One day now equals one month earlier relaxing on the beaches.

4 - A home based business where you can invest work and time instead of money.

You can make more money with a business of

your own than a job would pay you and the tax benefits are worth the effort. It would be a good practice to start slow and small and work it steadily. Eventually, the income will exceed your job and you will need to make a decision as to whether you want to quit your job and take your business full time.

Most people don't even bother to start anything, and then complain about others getting lucky. The guy who wrote a book and got rich all of a sudden, the youtuber who does the most stupid videos and earns millions of dollars annually. Sure, they might have been lucky, but it is their efforts that gave them the CHANCE to be lucky. Make your own luck, start your own business or sidegig. DO SOMETHING that allows you to get lucky.

5 - Residual vs. Linear Income

Most people work at a job that pays them a linear income, which means that for every hour they work they get paid an hour's wage. Or they sell a widget and get paid a commission on that one widget.

Residual income, on the other hand, is cumulative and continuous. Let's say that you sell a widget, instead of getting paid a onetime commission, you get an ongoing commission for that sale month after month. Sell two widgets, get two times the residual.

In today's booming internet world the sky is the limit, start producing valuable things and thinking about how to solve peoples problems. That is your key to success, find ways of income that are not dependant on your time. Don't exchange an hour for a fixed amount of money. Instead, invest hundreds of hours to do something that produces value which will, in return provide you with millions of hours back.

6 – Live frugally

Decrease costs like your life depends on it,

because it does. Don't try to fake being rich or living up to social media standards just for the sake of it. You are young now, nobody expects you to have an expensive car or luxury brands. Live like no-one today so you can live like no-one tommorow.

Always think twice about buying things you don't need, the best way of doing this is thinking about the amount of money you are spending now, and how much it will be worth after 20 years of investment on a humble 7% return rate. Suddenly that luxury bag worth 5,000$ invested for 20 years equals 20,000$ in 20 years.

Take that in, think about it and decide if it is really worth it right now.

7 - Positive Mental Attitude

I used to think that keeping a positive mental attitude was the key ingredient to success and achievement that if I maintained a PMA, success was sure to follow. I knew people that cranked up the positive attitude so much they glowed but were complete financial failures. Wealth & success aren't built by PMA. They aren't built by hard work. Being optimistic is not the key to becoming rich. You become rich by finding the most efficient financial plan customized to yourself and following it like your life depends on it.

Do the math, construct a plan, follow it. Doesn't matter if you are not feeling well and justify it by relieving 'stress' by going on a shopping spree. Do the math and Stick to it.

8 - Compound Interest

Compound interest refers to the fact that whenever interest is calculated, it is based not only on the original principal, but also on any unpaid interest that has been added to the principal. The more frequently interest is compounded, the faster the balance grows.

This is also called the eighth wonder of the word

by albert einstein. 1 dollar today is 4 dollars tommorow. 1 million today is 4million tommorow, get the hang of it?

Think of your money as small ant soldiers that go to war and bring more soldiers back, the more soldiers you have the more soldiers they get & this becomes a vicious cycle which forms a huge snowball that will spin your wealth to amounts you never even imagined you could get.

BASIC PRINCIPLES TO SEVEN FIGURE RETIREMENT

I would prefer you didn't throw eggs at the screen! It damages monitors and does nothing for your financial bottom line.

If you put $100.00 in a savings account for the next 12 years, from the time you turn 19, when you retire, you'll have a million bucks in the bank. Can you retire on seven figures? Probably not, but that's a good start on what you can retire on, plus I'm not here to tell you how to get rich at 65 or 70 years old.

There are some basic principles working in your life, and I want to share them with you. You may not realize they're working, but they are. And they work in your life, whether you work them, whether you know about them or not, and whether or not you believe in them. They're still working.

1: You have to GIVE to GET.

In our introductory book 'why giving more, gets you more' we go through this key point. You have to give more, to get more. Meaning You have to strive to make value & solve daily problems and money will follow suit.

Go look at the richest and most successful entrepeneurs around, they all have one thing in common. That is they have made our lives easier in someway or another.

Be for value, make it your goal to create something helpful and money will follow suit.

2: Integrity isn't optional.

Dishonesty will not take you anywhere in life. You must be honest. No a little bit honest. Not honest sometimes. Not honest when it's convenient. You MUST be HONEST. Without integrity, your life isn't worth the salt in your bread, and quite frankly, you aren't worth keeping. If you've been dishonest in the past, you can change, but DO IT NOW! Integrity isn't optional.

Nowadays marketing is all about scams, you can never trust anything you see on tv. In addition, even most people will tell you nowadays to 'fake it until you make it'.

Well guess what, you can't fake making a new iphone or facebook. You can't fake providing value. Sooner or later, it will come biting you right in the behind and cost you even more.

3: Pay yourself first.

Some of the outdated books will tell you 10%, no you will not be able to retire early with that percentage of savings rate.

ATLEAST 60% of everything you earn should go into a savings account that you don't touch. In fact, it should go into a savings account the minute you get paid. In fact, it should go into the savings account so fast that you don't even think about anything else you could do with that money. You should NOT touch that money for any reason. Why? Because it's savings. It's a requirement that you put it in and don't take it out. Leave it there and let it grow. That's why it's called SAVINGS. The only time you should touch these 'savings' are in two cases and TWO cases ONLY

1) Investing in assets that will generate more return on investment(ROI).

2) Check rule no.1.

RETIREMENT PLANNING

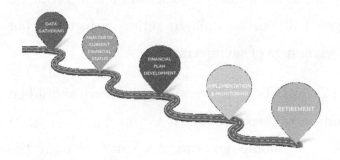

Everyone retires one day so the earlier you start your retirement planning, the better for your future. It really does not matter whether you would be retiring in the next 5 years or the next 20, start planning now. That would definitely improve your financial future and your chances to retire earlier.

The Need for Retirement Planning

People think of ideal retirement as a combination of leisure activities, financial independence and luxury vacations - all these things are possible only if you have enough money when you retire.

To live a comfortable life after you retire, you need financial planning. There are many tools and resources available to help you plan better.

People often debate this fact by saying 'You are only, young once', 'YOLO' - which translates to you only live once, but ask them this – does their life end today? this year? is tommorow or next year or even the 60 years left ahead of you not 'your life' that you only live once?

Nowadays the average life expectancy is 80+years old. Assuming you start at 30, Do you really want to enjoy 10 years to struggle 40years? or do you want to struggle 10 to enjoy 40?

The Basic Steps Of Retirement Planning

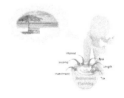

How much money would you need after you retire? - This is dependent on your current standard of living. You need to estimate what your annual expenses will be after you retire. One point to be taken into consideration for this estimation is the difference between the current expenses and retirement expenses. For example, right now a large percentage of your income goes towards your house mortgage and children's education. But by the time you retire, your children must have settled with their jobs and you would have a home of your own. When you retire, you and your spouse may have increased medical expenses and you would also like to spend money on vacations. Here, you also need to consider inflation. The average inflation rate is around 2 to 3%. That means in theory, if you don't invest your money and keep it in a savings account with 1.5 to 2% interest rate, you are actually LOSING money as time goes by.

How much would you need to save? - After you calculate the inflow that may come from part time income, interest on the investments and Social Security; you need to estimate the exact value that your assets will have and the income you will earn after you retire. By calculating this, you would come to know the shortfall. Here, there are many factors that need to be considered. At what age you are planning to retire, the number of years you are going to live (depends upon your health) and the return on your current investment. The first two factors roughly determine the number of years of your retirement. While calculating the rate of interest on your investment, take a conservative call and calculate the return based on around 5 to 6 percent. This would enable you to calculate the amount of money you require to save after you retire.

How to build the retirement corpus? - Once you have determined the amount of money needed to be saved each month from now till your retirement, the next step is to find a plan that is just right for your savings needs. Ideally, you should arrange for a specific amount that is directly taken from your monthly paycheck and automatically invested in the financial plan of your choice. This type of arrangement would reduce your impulsive spending habits. You can opt for payroll deduction savings plan or 401(k) plans.

For the perfect financial planning, you need to understand the different savings and investment options that are available to you. This definitely requires a lot of dedication on your part. If you are busy and can not find enough time or do not quite understand the intricacies of various investment plans then it is advisable to LEARN about them, and learn that most financial advisors take a small fee – which in theory becomes a LARGE sum after time. Financial security after you retire is important - you must start learning, educating yourself and planning for it now.

Tips For Achieving Financial Independence

Most of us seem to forget one of the most obvious things in our life even though it is that simple; money is only a tool to help us to do what we want, to live out your dreams or goals as far as money can by them. Have you ever considered to live on little money? You can even live well with little money but the biggest benefit of living on a small budget now, is that you will be able to live a life of leisure where you can spend your time and energy doing things that you choose to do within some years. To gain financial independence whether your purpose is retirement planning or another purpose, there is more than one way to go. Roughly there are three ways to obtain it: R.I.R

1. Reducing expenses

2. Increasing income

3 .Reducing spendings

This is obvious - but so many people have not understood it yet: Always spend less money than you make. Continually track and review your purchases for the purposes of keeping track of your money as well as learning from your previous mistakes. We are actually talking about a change in your lifestyle, and you can't expect to do this change overnight.

Never use money on impulses but always plan and prioritize your purchases. You must understand that money is not the important thing, the important thing is to have a good life. Therefore sit down and find out what is really important for you in your life and prioritize your use of money according to that. Focus on achieving your goal and never lose sight of it. Be creative and constantly look for ways to live well without much money. Who said you couldn't live a good life frugally?

When you plan to use money on items for your household like a dish washer, vacuum cleaner, refrigerator etc. only buy what you absolutely need and see that it lasts as long as possible. You must ask yourself: Will this item benefit me? You must continually go through a process of selecting strategic use of money as well as do all you can to save money on all your purchases.

If you owe money, make a debt elimination plan and stick to it This is especially important for consumer debt; get rid of it and the sooner the better. Why not move to the countryside. The point is that you should find a place to live that limits your expenses where you at the same time can live a good and healthy life.

Increase your income

If you don't already have it, you should find a job that pays well and doesn't add a lot of cost to your life. You should continually look at improving your income by getting a higher paying job

earning more side income.

The cost you save by changing your lifestyle - your surplus - should be invested. Keep investing the surplus and accumulate it. If you can come so far that you are able to invest $1,000 to $2,000 a month for 12 to 15 years or even better if you can increase your savings by a few percent each year, you will be able to withdraw a decent income from the interest on your investment.

It is possible to re-engineer your life to live well even on little money. If a financial emergency should occur, it is necessary to have some money available. Therefore your should establish and maintain an emergency fund. The more income you make, the more money you can save with a frugal lifestyle. If your goal is to retire, remember that the more income you can get and the lower expenses you have, the quicker you can retire. If you get used to living on a moderate amount of money and prioritize what you really want to do, as far as what money can buy, you will be the master of your time and money - in other words you will be in control of your life.

GOAL FOR SUCCESS

Have you ever imagined setting out on a journey without knowing exactly where your destination is? Can you also think of a ship venturing into the high seas with the captain not knowing where it is heading? Chances of getting to any destination are slim and it will probably get lost at sea. Consider another ship whose skipper has a map and all the navigational aids. He cannot see his faraway destination, but he can show you exactly where he is heading on the map and his route. At any point in the journey, the skipper can tell you precisely his location.

A survey carried out in the United States some years ago, showed that only 5 per cent of all Americans interviewed could explain in clear terms what their goal in life was. Most of them revealed that they went to work to support their families and make a living. In other words, they just wanted to get by and live an average life, doing what relatives, friends and neighbors were also doing. Another survey conducted showed that most Americans were not financially independent at age 65. Many of them in fact went broke in the world's richest country.

Why is this so? The reason is simple. Most people do not have a clear goal in life. This is not just an American but a worldwide problem. It is not an accident that less than 10 per cent of people are financially independent at age 65 when they should be retiring into comfort for the rest of their lives.

Almost everyday in the news media, you will read about or watch the news of someone who overcame one obstacle or handicap to achieve greatness. The stories of the legendary Henry Ford, the pioneer car manufacturer and Thomas Edison, who invented the electric bulb, should serve as inspiration. Both men did not complete high school; but they had one thing in common a goal.

Only recently, I watched a young man on the Oprah Winfrey Show. He had lost both legs while mountaineering in Australia. When asked if he would ever attempt to climb any mountain, he quickly responded that he was going back to the same mountain in Australia. He felt the mountain had challenged him by denying him two his legs. The young climber promised to get back there as early as possible, because he would like to be a role model for all handicapped people. That was his goal in life. Meanwhile, he was traveling around the United States in his prosthesis, encouraging the physically handicapped to go ahead to realize their dreams, against all odds.

The world is replete with stories of people who had to overcome great difficulty to achieve their life's goals. Goal setting is not all however. You must also stick to your goal; always focus on it. Always keep the big picture in your mind and like the ship's captain, keep a mental sea map.

Thus, setting a goal for yourself is the surest way to achieving success. This is true whether you are a single individual or a corporation. You are aware that no corporation can operate or succeed without setting a goal.

SEVEN MASTER WEALTH CREATION

Millionaire income level is developed all the same way. To become a millionaire, and develop a mastering of wealth creation strategy is fundamentally based on the same seven steps. Every day I start out reviewing my goals and plan to develop financial security. Even during these troubled economic conditions there are ways of mastering wealth creation. You just need to be prepared for the opportunities to generate wealth when they present themselves. Here are seven steps to mastering wealth creation and become a millionaire.

1. Get your act together. Decide that you are going to change the way things are today and change them. You have to make a decision that you want to become wealthy first to become wealthy, this is a mind-set. Eliminate all the negativity that surrounds you and get your act together. Don't let the distractions of life continue to force you off course. Set your goals and act on them.

2. Get yourself focused on the prize you wish to achieve. No matter what your goals are stay focused. Sure there may be obstacles along the way, and sure you may have challenges to overcome along the way, stay focused! Nothing else should matter but putting in motion a specific plan to achieve your goals that you set up as the ultimate reward and satisfaction of mastering wealth creation. Everything you do in the course of your day should be action toward achieving your goals. If you really want to create a million dollar income and become a millionaire, you are your own worst enemy and without the focus and commitment, to your goal you will not succeed.

3. Get control of your finances. Nothing could be more important than this step, no matter where you are in your plan to create more wealth, you need to evaluate your current financial situation, begin to reduce any frivolous debt, control outgoing expenditures, and regain control of your finances. Yes the old saying is true today as it was in days past, "it takes money to make money." get control of your finances, establish an operating budget, stick to it everyday, freeing up the necessary capital to put forth to build a lucrative cash generating business.

4. Develop a 'positive mental attitude'. Stop for a minute and think, have you ever met a wealthy person that was just miserable because they were wealthy. NO! Most successful people have a great positive mental attitude towards life, and usually share this with others in their acts of kindness and generosity towards there fellow man. Stop reading the crap in the newspapers and on the internet about how bad things are. Stop watching the news, or listening to others about how tough things are right now. Get into reading books and articles about how to improve your self, be happy and positive and you will attack your plan to mastering wealth creation with more vigor and energy than ever before.

5. Have faith in yourself. Everyone is born with the same skill sets and opportunities to succeed right from birth. Tap into these reserves and stop doubting that you are not as worthy or as deserving as any man that created wealth on this planet has ever been. Most people trudge through life thinking that they were dealt a bad hand, or just don't have what it takes. If you're knocked down, Get up! Dust yourself off, and get to work. Have faith that you can master anything you put your mind to, you just have to have the faith in yourself to do so!

6. Browse the money "vehicles" If you already know what yours is, so much the better. You're ready to move forward. if not, do some due diligence to make a sound choice to move forward in your quest to become wealthy. Your money vehicle should be something you can be passionate about, something you can obsess over every waking minute of every day. This "vehicle" should be a driving force that excites you and drives you. This will be the business that will provide the wealth for you as you strive to build it to a multi-million dollar brand.

7. Begin your practical education and training. Once you've selected your path for achieving wealth plug into the training and education needed to develop the expertise to be able to master wealth creation. Access any mode of educating yourself to consume the information to create wealth in the field you have chosen. Find mentors that have gone before you, attend classes and webinars, take positions in relevant arenas to grasp first hand knowledge. Learn as much information necessary to gain confidence in your plan of action to succeed! Review everything you learn from all the courses and systems, choose one, apply it, and commit yourself to just doing it no matter what.

HABITS THAT BUILD FINANCIAL INDEPENDENCE

Financial independence is having the freedom to support yourself through your own efforts. Here are seven fundamental habits that will help you achieve and maintain financial independence.

1. Express Gratitude

Financial independence begins with gratitude. Set aside a daily period to offer a sincere thank you for every blessing in your life. Include people, places, possessions, talents, and memories. Offer gratitude for your future dreams as though they were already in your possession.

Gratitude will allow you to attract the blessings you want. When they arrive, protect them with your life from anything that could rob you of your financial independence. This is also known as wealth preservation.

2. Liberate Your Future

Debts of the past are thieves of the future. If you want financial independence, live a simple life style that does not create unnecessary personal debt. Living with class does not require being extravagant. If you are conservative most of the time, you can be extravagant at the right times.

Do not allow credit card companies to hold your future hostage. Take control. Seek professional help to get rid of credit card debt that robs you of high monthly interest payments. Borrowing is a tool that should produce a return on your investment, not cost your future security.

Make it a rule to only borrow money when you are using it to increase your assets, which produce income. Never ever borrow money for liabilities, that chip away from your money and your hard work.

3. Commit to Wellness

Your health is also an asset that you need to protect. Wellness allows you to manage and enjoy financial independence. Get regular physical checkups and maintain a sensible physician-approved exercise program. These can help to minimize illnesses and maximize the rewards of a productive life.

Maintaining wellness requires an ongoing commitment. Another area of commitment that is equally important to financial independence is one of personal financial discipline.

A check up for 100$ today can cost you medical bills of over 10,000$ in the future. Your health is most important and you should invest in it.

4. Develop a Saving Discipline

A financially independent future requires saving, and saving requires discipline. As credit card debt diminishes, savings can begin to increase. An emergency savings fund of three to six months living expenses is a wise idea. However, you will want major long-term savings plans for such goals as education and retirement.

Do not expect the government to take care of your financial future. If you want to remain financially independent, take ultimate responsibility for every chapter of your financial life. That responsibility begins with wise investing and respect for money.

5. Invest Wisely and Respect Money

A wise man once taught me to have several investments that produce an ongoing, passive income. This, he said, would allow me to remain independent if I were to become physically disabled. These investments are like "feeding geese that lay golden eggs". Passive income streams also provide additional capital to place in other financial growth investments.

Respect for money is the beginning of saving and investing. Respect for a dollar begins with respect for a penny. You will always have dollars if you take care of your pennies. Even the smallest of assets and investments need protection.

An easy way to begin respecting your money is thinking about it in a percentage, not sums. For example, say you have a choice to buy something you need one is 5$ and one is 5.5$. Here most people would choose whatever they prefer and often choose the higher priced one since it's 'only 0.5$ more' - even if they don't need the upgrade.

But if you think of it that the 0.5$ is actually 10% of the whole amount, suddenly it doesn't look so small. You would have to invest 5$ for 5 years in a savings account to get that 0.5$ back(assuming 2% interest rate). Suddenly it doesn't look so small now – Learn to treat and think of your money in percentages.

6. Protect Yourself and Your Loved Ones

Ten Traits of Successful Entrepreneurs, I wrote that one of those traits was making a commitment to protect the welfare of your family and loved ones. Ensuring the safety of your financial assets is part of doing this.

Adequate insurance coverage for your life, health, and property is a wise investment. You should also use professional legal, financial, and security services to help protect your business, property, and all the things you have worked to acquire.

A good rule of thumb is that your insurances shouldn't exceed 5% of your monthly income.

7. Design Your Financial Independence with Qualified Help

Seek qualified professionals to help you design your financial future. You do not need to be a financial expert to become financially independent, but you must become financially literate. Seek professional guidance from experts in financial planning, taxes, and accounting. These people can work with you to help you realize your financial goals.

Begin today by seeking out professionals that can help you achieve your financial goals. Become financially independent in your own mind. Express gratitude for the blessings you will receive as if they were already in your possession. Avoid and eliminate unnecessary personal debt, and live a healthy lifestyle. Save with discipline, invest wisely, and respect your financial assets. Protect the assets you have worked to acquire, and you can enjoy the financially independent lifestyle that you have envisioned.

FINANCIAL INDEPENDENCE AND PHILOSOPHY

The FIRE movement has gained a lot of traction over the last decade. FIRE stands for financial independence, retire early. In its core the movement revolves around saving and investing in order to retire way earlier than traditional budgets would allow. The goal is to live solely off passive income combined with small withdrawals from a investment portfolio. You don't need to work to maintain your lifestyle.

A typical guideline is achieving a portfolio of 25 to 30 times your annual expenses and withdraw 3%-4% annually to cover living expenses. The target portfolio and withdrawal rate depends on your desired lifestyle.

Types of FIRE

There are different approaches on how to become financially independent and retire early. It's important understand the route of financial independence is not set in stone. What FIRE type fits you, your family and lifestyle best?

The most common approaches to FIRE are:

"Fat FIRE" refers to a more traditional lifestyle who saves more than the average retirement investor.

"Lean FIRE" refers to a frugal lifestyle and extreme savings, resulting in a far more restricted lifestyle.

"Barista FIRE" refers to a person who has quit their traditional 9-to-5 job, but still undertakes some form of part-time work to cover for living expenses.

How aggressive is being saved and invested is a key difference in how the FIRE philosophy is put into practise. I recommend calculating your own FI numbers / passive income numbers and play around with the monthly contribution to your investment portfolio. This gives you a good understanding of the road ahead.

Accumulating wealth

The accumulating wealth phase is critical in any plan to attain financial independence. Being able to speed up the accumulation or growing phase will allow you hit your FI target faster and 'retire' sooner. Therefore it's helpful understanding what the main variables are for building your investment portfolio.

1. Income

Income is a key variable for growing your portfolio. Increasing take-home income while keeping your expenses unchanged allows you to save more. More savings means bigger contributions to your investment portfolio. As a result you could be ending up shaving off years from your retirement date. Remember one day today is worth a month later, one month today may shave an year off in the future.

2. Expenses

A second variable for growing your portfolio are expenses. Reducing expenses means higher savings and as a result bigger contributions to your investment portfolio. At the same time cutting annual expenses also means you can reduce your FI target. Effectively a double win. It's recommended to track and categorize your expenses in order to understand how you're spending your money.

Become obsessed with your personal finance and track every cent. Remember, saving 200$ a month might be equal to increasing your income by 10% MONTHLY, and that truly is the best investment you can do right now.

3. Return on investment

The return on your investment portfolio is the third criteria which determines the pace at which you're able to accumulate wealth. The higher the return, the faster your portfolio grows. It's essential to understand the power of compound interest in connection to your investment portfolio. Compound interest is a mechanism that'll propel you towards financial independence.

Don't spend those monthly passive incomes once you get them, invest them back. The point here is not to be able to get your pets snack money monthly. But to be able to retire infinitely without the need to work forever. Compound interest will not work if you keep spending the monthly passive income you get without reinvesting it back.

4. Time

Time itself is not a variable in order to accumulate wealth faster. The reason 'Time" is worth mentioning is its relation with compound interest. Accumulating wealth becomes increasingly easier over time. The larger your portfolio, the more compound interest is able to show its true potential.

Therefore it's advisable to start saving and investing early on in life. Always remember, now is the earliest you can start in your life. Even if you fail to retire early, make sure you can live the rest of your life happily without financial concerns – and by doing that will you only be able to truly enjoy life.

financial independence

A savings rate of 64% allows you to achieve financial independence in 10.9 years, assuming 5% annual returns, and that is a modest annual return. Again, if you can't increase your income increase your savings, even a 1% increase of savings will matter in the long run – 1% today equals 10% tomorrow.

Investment strategies

Browsing through FIRE forums and blogs you'll typically encounter the same set of investment strategies being used to reach financial independence. The three strategies appearing most often are investing in the stock market with index funds, investing in real estate and investing in crowdlending platforms(p2p). It's perfectly viable to combine strategies as well, and I usually recommend diversifying your portfolio adjusted to your risk tolerance and personal circumstances.

Index funds

The average investor will not manage to outperform the stock market, but should instead aim to BE the market. Index funds are a great way to become the market. Key advantages of index funds are the ease of diversification, the utilization of compound interest from dividend yields and its expected returns on the long term.

When selecting an index fund it's advised to carefully consider its cost ratio and exposure. As mentioned in the paragraph on accumulating wealth, return on investment is a key variable for growing your portfolio. Well diversified low cost index funds are typically recommended for the average investor. Vanguard is widely recognized as a solid choice, but there are many more options out there.

Remember, don't try to find the needle in the haystack. Buy the haystack instead of failing constantly trying to find that precious little gem.

Real Estate

Real Estate has been a popular asset class for a long time, and for good reason. The options for building wealth with real estate are plentiful. Common strategies include value appreciation, generating rental income and flipping properties for profit.

Remember, location is most important and nowadays, competition has never been tougher. I'd advise of 1) investing in rural areas or cities far from your capital city. 2) You only need one or two good finds to success – take your time and pick wisely.

FIRE philosophy and investment choice

My personal belief is that financial independence is achievable for anyone and is not reserved for a select few. The simple math doesn't lie. Spend less than you earn, invest the difference and compound your way to financial independence.

I do recognize the pace at which FI is achievable is not identical for everyone. Bigger incomes will have an easier time to reach a higher savings rate. Always keep in mind reaching FI is not a competition, but a journey. And this journey is different for everyone. The key is deciding to get started.

Journey

Financial independence represents freedom for me. The freedom to choose how I spend my time. Quite frankly, I have no intention of retiring completely and I do enjoy my current job. But it's not the same as having complete freedom over your time and I feel that's worth attaining. Combine that thought with a desire to spend more time traveling and having the choice to really see my future kids grow up.

The biggest pet peve I have is people saying that is impossible and they will never be millionaires. That is true, not with your current lifestyle. But, remember the average person lives over 80 years old. You still have half of your life left where you will be old, weak & probably not able to work for income anymore. Start changing your life now, do the maths and you WILL realize it is actually in fact, possible.

HAVING THE CONFIDENCE TO RETIRE EARLY

I have been recommending that a certain couple should retire early for a few years. I am pleased to say that they have now taken the plunge and made the decision to do so. They can afford to retire, but the decision was delayed by them not having the confidence to retire early.

How did we convince them to retire early?

We showed them the effect of their lifestyle on their assets and income in the future by preparing a comprehensive financial plan. This removed all the complexities of all those products, and showed them in a straightforward way the implications of their lifestyle decisions.

The clients' main issue was 'will I run out of money if I stop working too soon?' We were able to demonstrate to them that this was not the case - therefore they could afford to retire now. This is the power of financial planning. We can look at what is important to you, and then apply this to different scenarios to show you the effects of your future planned lifestyle. In this case, we showed them what would happen if they continued on to work until their original planned retirement date. We then examined how their finances would change if they stopped working a number of years earlier and started spending sooner.

The issues to consider with early retirement

The obvious positive is that you should be making the most of your life which you are still fit enough to enjoy it. We all know stories of people who worked hard for many years, but could not enjoy their later years due to illness or early death. Therefore, we should aim to make the most of our remaining time while we still can, and that means looking to retire earlier. Of course, what tends to hold people back is not being able to see the big picture; without the confidence a financial plan can bring, it if difficult to take the plunge because of the fear of getting the decision wrong.

If you retire early you will have less time to accumulate assets, and you will drain the ones you have faster because you will spend the money sooner and quicker. Also, we all know that the cost of living tends to go up, especially for retired people. This means that the decision to retire early can have a drastic effect on your future prosperity, and therefore your ability to live the life you want. Only by knowing how these issues affect your lifestyle can you make a decision to become financially independent and therefore stop working.

Early Retirement

Does the idea of finally escaping from the anxiety and frustration of the workplace cause you to salivate? How about being able to sleep until you wake up naturally? The joy of freely coming and going as we please, is a great luxury and one that is highly prized by most people.

Early Retirement For Health

As we grow older, physical considerations make retiring early a desirable position. Some may be forced to retire early for health reasons. Even for people who have perfect health, normally the physical demands of working become less enjoyable as we age.

You don't have to be a senior citizen to dream of relaxing within a leisurely, abundant lifestyle. What young person has not dreamed of fine cars and plenty of free time to enjoy them?

Whatever the reason for desiring to retire prematurely, one thing is an absolute pre-requisite. What is that one thing you ask, well of course it is MONEY.

Proper planning can provide an adequate income for that golden period.

Three essential elements of making this dream a reality are:

- Income Earned

- Time

- Investment Knowledge

Early Retirement Income

We have been blessed with the potential to earn enough to be able to spend part of our life without working or working as we choose. Obviously, this possibility is very much based on the amount of income we earn during our productive work years.

Time is a great ally of the younger person who wishes to one day be free to enjoy the fruit of his labors. Thirty years gives a younger person plenty of time to accumulate a sizeable wealth portfolio with the added benefit of compounding investments. BUT, it is never too late to make corrections in our planning. There is always time to make progress, make improvements in our plan and move toward our goal of financial freedom.

Early Retirement Strategy

So, we have worked hard and used time to our advantage. We have a little wealth, maybe a lot of wealth, but now what do we do? How many famous people have we heard of who made millions of dollars a year and are now broke? Time and Income Earned are wasted if we do not hang on to a sufficient portion of our earnings for retiring. This is why the third essential element of any good retiree program consist of investment knowledge

TYPES OF RETIREMENT INVESTMENTS FOR A STEADY STREAM OF INCOME

As you near your 60's, your prime earning and saving years will transition into a period of time where you get to enjoy the "fruits of your labor," a.k.a retirement. We call this segueing from accumulation to decumulation, the period when you will be drawing from your accumulated nest egg. You need to find the best retirement investments so that you can generate regular income, without having to go back to work. Here's an overview of the most popular income-producing retirement investments.

1) Immediate Annuities

Immediate annuities provide guaranteed income immediately (hence the name). They are a form of insurance rather than an investment (but still included here because they provide steady income). A ten-year term-certain annuity, for example, buys a stream of income for ten years. Because immediate annuities start paying out right away, they appeal to people already retired. They are not for everyone – they tie up assets, and you may "lose" money if you die before fully "cashing out." Immediate annuities may be advantageous if you have trouble staying within your spending limits, cannot stick to an investment plan, or have no monthly sources of income besides Social Security.

2) Bonds

Bonds, individual or bundled in funds, are loans you give to governments, municipalities or corporations that then pay you regular interest. When the bond matures, its face value is returned to you. We often recommend clients purchase bonds in a bond ladder, which is a collection of bonds that have different maturity dates set to match their future cash flow needs. Bonds are a lower-risk option than other investments, which means lower returns (usually). Buy bonds not to grow money but for the regular interest income they produce, and for the guaranteed principal you will receive when they mature.

3) Retirement Income Funds

Retirement income funds are great for folks who aren't interested in keeping regular tabs on their portfolio. They are a type of mutual fund; they automatically invest your money in a diversified portfolio of stocks and bonds. The fund's goal is to produce monthly income. Most people have experience with mutual funds, so they feel comfortable with retirement income funds. And, like mutual funds, retirement income funds are set up so you can access your money at any time.

4) Rental Real Estate

Renting out property for income requires a hands-on approach, and in many cases, more work than you might have anticipated for your golden years. Research and forethought are key. Before you decide to become a landlord in retirement, consider the rental property expenses you may incur over the time-frame you plan to own the property, like maintenance, damage from negligent renters, natural disasters, etc. You also need to factor in vacancy rates—no property remains rented 100 percent of the time. For those with a real estate background, or if you want to put the time in, real estate can be a great source of regular income but go in with your eyes wide open.

5) Real Estate Investment Trusts (REITs)

A REIT (Real Estate Investment Trust) is a mutual fund that aggregates real estate holdings (apartment buildings, commercial structures, vacation properties, etc.). For a fee, professionals manage the properties, collect rent, and pay expenses, and you receive the remaining income. As part of a diversified portfolio, REITs can be a good retirement investment choice.

6) Variable Annuity With a Lifetime Income Rider

Variable annuities are complicated. In a variable annuity, your money goes into a portfolio of investments you choose. For a fee, you can add an optional benefit, called a rider. The rider insures the amount of future income you can withdraw from your portfolio. Variable annuities come in many flavors, and many people who offer them don't truly understand them. Be cautious – sometimes I see variable annuities with total fees running about three to four percent (ouch!) a year. Your investments will have to earn back the fees and more for you to benefit.

7) Closed-End Funds

Not for newbie investors, closed-end funds encompass a wide range of investment approaches that may be unfamiliar to the layman (they overlay stocks and bonds with strategies like dividend captures and covered calls). Income comes from interest, dividends, premiums from selling options like covered calls, or return of principal. Some closed-end funds use leverage (they borrow against the portfolio) —an additional risk that is employed to buy more income-producing securities so the fund can pay an overall higher yield. Closed-end funds can be a great retirement investment option, as part of a mix, for savvy investors.

8) Dividend Income Funds

A dividend income fund, like other funds, is a

collection of stocks overseen by a fund manager. The dividends you receive come from the dividends paid out by the underlying stocks in the fund. Dividends can rise one year and fall the next. Some publicly-traded companies generate qualified dividends, which are taxed at a lower rate than other income. As such, it may be most tax-efficient to hold qualified dividends within non-retirement accounts (meaning not inside of an IRA, Roth IRA, 401(k), etc.). I caution clients to be wary of funds that advertise high yields – yields that are higher than average typically come with additional risks.

9) Total Return Portfolio

When done right, a total return portfolio is one of the best retirement investments out there. It is not a stand-alone investment; it is a strategy that uses a balanced, diverse blend of stock and bond index funds that provide retirement income in the form of interest, dividends, and capital gains. The portfolio is designed to achieve a respectable long-term rate of return, and along the way, you follow a prescribed set of withdrawal rate rules that will typically allow you to take out 4-7 percent a year, and in some years, increase your withdrawal for inflation. What does "total return" mean? Well, unlike a Certificate of Deposit, that has a specific interest rate, with a total return portfolio you don't know what the actual return will be each year. Some years your investments could be up 14%, and other years down -10%. But you know over a ten-year span of time that a specific mix of investments, such as 60% stock index funds and 40% bonds, has a high probability of earning a 6-7% average rate of return. So you are targeting that "total" average return, rather than knowing the exact outcome each year.

Keep in mind many of the vehicles discussed above are investment products, not financial planning tools. Many financial advisors are salespeople who place too much emphasis on investment selection and investment products and too little on the risks that come with it.

SECRETS ON HOW TO RETIRE A MILLIONAIRE

The idea of becoming rich in life is often a daydream to most people, but those who have the drive to pursue it can reach financial prosperity. The greatest thing to know is that if you don't find out what the rich do, you may not be able to make your first million dollars and retire at an early age. Here, you would discover rare secrets on how to retire a millionaire with little cash.

What actually make the rich different from the poor? It's simply what they know that you don't know.

Setting a Financial Goal Early in Life

It's quite an interesting thing to retire at an age in which you can enjoy your fruits of hard work. There is no point in accumulating wealth that might eventually be a provision for your burial ceremony. Well, that's on a lighter mood, yet it's a simple truth. In respect of this subject of how to retire a millionaire at 40, you would find out that the idea of setting a personal financial goal should be in the mind of every young one. Nevertheless, you can still apply the secrets to your life at any age. Depending on the business you do, about 10 - 20 years would be required to achieve this goal in life.

Millionaire Mindset

You need to inculcate the millionaire mindset by taking an honest look at your present financial situation. Wealth is first a state of the mind before it becomes a state of life. Change any bad spending habits that make you lose the sum of money you could have otherwise saved or invested for your retirement age.

Assess and Classify Your Debt

Where are you in debt? Is it a good, debt, or a bad debt? The former includes acquiring mortgage property which appreciates in value while the latter includes a new car (it has a depreciating value). The worst kind of debt is that of credit card usage which can make you to live above your means. It's even tempting to have a good credit rating as this might make you to seek for more offers from credit card companies, and it might get to a level where you won't be able to pay off all your debts totally. If you are already in debt, pay it off and start to save and invest.

Save and Invest Money

Do you know that money has time value? The money you save today won't have the same value tomorrow. If you spend the money you should have saved today, you have eaten a portion of your future. Consistent saving of money will help you to reach your financial goal. Many people don't understand that it takes little cash to invest and retire a millionaire. Three things are important - the average saving amount, the money-saving period, and the interest rate. Based on the assumption that you're now 20 years old with a financial goal of accumulating $1 million at 40, at 8% interest, you would be expected to save an estimated sum of $10,000 - $15,000 per year, that is, an average of $1000 per month. If you want to make 1 million dollars at 60, you'd only need around $400 - $500 per month at the same interest rate.

Making the $1000/Month for Your Investment

In order to reach the $1 million mark, it's quite imperative that you have a consistent source of income. Except you belong to any of the high-paying working classes such as the nurses and doctors, it might be difficult to set aside as much as $1000 to $2000 per month in order to reach $1 million by the age of 40, assuming you start at the age of 20. From the foregoing, you only have 20 years to meet the financial goal. Practically speaking, the best way to retire a millionaire at 40 in such a case is to opt for highly profitable online opportunities.

Here are some businesses that have helped some people become Internet millionaires:

Information Marketing

Affiliate Marketing

Virtual Company

SEO Services

E-commerce

Multi-level Marketing Businesses

Adopting any of the above businesses would be of great help to you. In fact, if you have a good business plan, you can make a $1 million between 5 - 10 years. You would probably retire very rich. Try to research the suggested businesses to find the one that suits your passion and skills. Now that you know how to retire a millionaire at 40, you only need to take action, starting now, even if you are already above 20 years of age.

RULES THAT GUARANTEE FINANCIAL INDEPENDENCE

This simple rule is no more simple than the rules for guaranteeing that you achieve financial independence; that is, if financial independence is important to you. A wise man instilled in me that I should rely on no one certainly not the government if I wanted to live in my old age as well as I had lived when I was working.

There was a time when many workers in my age group thought that we could depend on Social Security to fund our retirement, but today we all should realize that possibility is unrealistic.

There is one simple rule for guaranteeing your FINANCIAL INDEPENDENCE: Start Early. While it is relatively easy to secure your financial future when you start building your next egg while you're in your twenties, it's next to impossible if you wait until you're in your fifties to start, but regardless of your age, begin immediately.

You don't have to be a financial genius to be financially independent; I am living proof of this fact. But you do have to develop the discipline to follow a few simple rules. I learned these rules from the very best and the very brightest. These rules are FREE. Follow them and your financial future is virtually guaranteed.

1. The secret to financial independence is the understanding of the basic principle of COMPOUNDING OF WEALTH. If you don't grasp this principle, you will most likely have to win the Powerball Lottery to be independently wealthy.

The main key to financial success is forcing yourself to live on 40% to 50% (50% to 60% for investing) of your take-home income and invest each month the 50% that you didn't spend.

As an example, the stock market has increased at a compounded rate of approximately 11% per year over the last 100 years. So $1,000 invested in, say, 1963 it would have been worth $88,897 by 2006.

Even if I had invested just $500 (10% of take-home pay in 1963), that investment would have been worth $44,449 in 2006.

Now, think about what you'd be worth if you invested $1,000 every year between your present age and 65 years of age. Wow! Becoming financially independent is really easy when you start early.

Here are some more rules:

2. Minimize your investments in assets that depreciate.

Automobiles, as an example, are essential for most of us, but they are lousy investments. A new car or truck that costs you $25,000 will depreciate approximately $2,500 to $5,000 in the first year of ownership. Those of us who feel the need to drive prestige cars, i.e., a Mercedes, BMW, Lexus, etc., will suffer $5,000 to $10,000 a year ($400 to $800 per month) in depreciation.

If you can live with driving a pre-owned car, you'll reduce both the investment itself and the portion of your investment that disappears via depreciation each month.

Other examples of depreciable assets are furniture and clothes. No matter how much you pay for these two assets, they will be worth next to nothing after just a few days of use.(I am being kind by calling them depreciable 'assets' as they should be called liabilities.)

3. Maximize your investment in assets that appreciate.

Over the long haul, most investments in real estate, i.e., your home, stocks, bonds, etc., will grow in value. So if you can discipline yourself to maximize your investments in these kinds of investments and minimize your investments in "fluffy" kinds of assets, you're much more likely to realize financial independence before it's too late.

4. Do your very best to pay cash and except for a first mortgage on your home, AVOID DEBT like it's the plague. This means paying off your credit cards each month, paying cash for furniture and automobiles, etc., to avoid unnecessary interest expense.

5. Establish a personal spending budget and live within it. There is no better tool for controlling spending and living within your income than developing the discipline to live by a spending budget.

When many people begin their business careers, and begin for the first time to generate some discretionary income, they go a little bit nuts. They spend everything they earn and then some. Perhaps the first sign of trouble is when they begin to generate credit card debt that they don't have the income to pay off each month. So they begin making the minimum payment, paying exorbitant rates of interest and digging a deeper hole for themselves each month.

The first step is to recognize what is happening, but the second step is to force yourself to plan your spending so that it doesn't exceed your after-tax income. I believe strongly that a budget should include an expense category for both saving and investing.

HOW TO BECOME A MILLIONAIRE

A Step by Step Guide to Making a Million Dollars

Becoming a millionaire is not extremely difficult. It takes money, time, discipline, and a little luck. All you need to do is follow these 5 steps:

You Need a Source of Income

Unless you are born into riches, inherit wealth, or strike it rich in the lottery, you need to earn money. You don't need to earn a lot of money to become wealthy; it's what you do with that money that matters.

If you want to increase your odds of becoming a millionaire, then look at some of these methods of making extra money. Just adding a few of these ideas to your lifestyle can increase your wealth. Check out a quick way to make an extra $250 free money just by opening up a new account with some of the online brokers who give out free stocks, you have to start somewhere!

Not only do you need a source of income, but having a second income is a great idea as well. I don't mean that you have to have an additional part-time job, but find a way to make a couple of extra bucks on the weekends or a few nights during the week. This could be anything from freelance work to selling homemade goods on Ebay. Making an extra hundred bucks every month could have a huge impact on your millionaire journey. It may not seem like a lot, but it can really add up every year.

How are we doing? My wife and I earn a decent living, but along the way, we made several lifestyle choices which reduced our income, including the decision for my wife to be a stay at home wife. I firmly believe we will still become millionaires – even in a one income household – and the reason I hold firm in this belief is that we follow the rest of the steps in this book.

Earn More Than You Spend

My wife and I have done fairly well with our finances, primarily because we spend less than we earn. Another, and perhaps better, way to look at this is to earn more than you spend. I am not implying you should deprive yourself of the things you enjoy or live a monk's lifestyle.

My belief is that you should focus on buying value on the things you enjoy, and you should focus on making big wins to reduce your expenses on non-essentials and things which don't bring you joy. For example, in our family eating out is a treat. We save a lot of money by not dining very often. This makes it more special in a way and allows my wife and I to enjoy the meal more.

Above all else, living within your means is the key to financial success. If you can combine both of these principles, earning more and spending less, you will be ahead of 95% of the world. If you want to supercharge your millionaire journey, it's important that you aren't spending every dime that you earn.

You probably can't demand a raise from your boss, but there are a few simple ways that you can essentially give yourself a raise. Simple cutting out some of your major expenses, like canceling your netflix or going out to eat less can save you hundreds of dollars every year. If you save $200 every month, you'll find yourself with $2,400 at the end of the year.

Save Some of Your Income

There is a simple fact that many people miss: you will never grow wealthy if you spend everything you earn. Regardless of how much money you earn, you need to put some aside in savings. Having a cash cushion is nice because it helps you prepare for unexpected expenses and helps you avoid debt. But there is another reason that saving money is important – because of taxes and other factors, money saved is worth more than money earned!

Another advantage of having some cash savings is the ability to use the money for investments or other large purchases when you come across a good deal. This could be a something like an investment, property, or just a good deal that saves you thousands of dollars on a major purchase. Take advantage of these principles and save money whenever possible.

Make Regular Investments

Investing is the best way to grow your wealth. Compound interest has been called the strongest force in the universe, and you want that force working for you! There are many ways to invest, and you can be successful as long as you make wise investment decisions and let time and compound interest work for you.

Investing in tax-advantaged retirement accounts such as a 401k or Roth IRA can help you grow your wealth more quickly since you won't have the drag of taxes pulling down your investment portfolio. You can also use retirement accounts to shape your taxes both now and in the future, giving you a powerful tool to help grow your wealth.

Investing can seem intimidating if you haven't started yet. But it doesn't have to be. Most people do the mistake of thinking that the higher interest rate that you get the riskier the investment is, this is in fact very wrong, and by increasing your financial knowledge will you only realize that yourself, As it is a fact that YOU must teach yourself and anyone else who would try to tell you this would seem like a scam artist or intruding in your 'personal' affairs.

Monitor and Repeat the Process

The path to becoming a millionaire becomes easier once you get the process started. It all starts at the beginning with small lifestyle changes. For example, making small lifestyle changes to reduce your fixed monthly expenses can go a long way toward helping you spend less than you earn. This, in turn, makes it easier to save a little money each month. Once you have a little cash saved, small emergencies are no longer emergencies and you are no longer treading water. This makes it easier to invest.

There are other things you can do to make the process easier. You can, for example, set up an automatic savings or investment program so you don't have to think about it. Out of sight, out of mind is a great motto when it comes to saving.

But you also need to know where your money is going. I recommend using some form of money tracking software to give you an idea of where your money is going. There are a number of excellent free online money management tools which make it easy to see your income, expenses, and spending patterns in one place.

My favorite is a free money management tool called Personal Capital which helps you track income, spending, and your investments.

Once you know your patterns, you can plan your spending and investing around them to help you reach your goals.

The Millionaire Mindset

Many of us are interested in becoming millionaires. However, that goal sometimes seems rather far away. You don't have to be born rich, or inherit a fortune, to become a millionaire. If you have the right stuff, you can work your way into your millions. But it helps to know what traits often make a millionaire. Here are 5 traits that many millionaires have and that you can develop:

1. Frugality

Not all millionaires are frugal. However, many of those who are self-made millionaires practice some form of frugality. Even billionaires like Warren Buffett have some frugal habits. Frugality is about look for ways to get the best value for your money. It doesn't always mean getting the cheapest thing; it's more about the best value. It also means that you don't waste your money on things that you don't need or want. Practicing frugality can help you keep more of your money for the future.

2. Willing to Make Wise Investments

Most millionaires know that it takes money to make money. Millionaires understand the power of compound interest. The study out how to make wise investments. Whether it's taking good care of themselves so that they aren't spending money on health care later, investing in a good education (not necessarily college, though), starting a business, or finding solid stocks to buy, millionaires study out what is likely to bring them a return. They make solid investments after considering the options.

3. Focus and Discipline

If you want to be a millionaire, it helps to know what you want, and then have the discipline to go after it. When you set a goal, you focus on it and pursue it. This means that you don't get sidetracked by less important matters. If you know that you need to set $1,000 a month aside in order to meet your millionaire goal within an allotted timeframe, you focus on that. You cut expenses or, better yet, look for ways to increase your income, so that you can meet your goal. Sometimes it's not fun, but millionaires usually stick with it.

4. Optimism

You might find, when speaking with millionaires — especially self-made millionaires — that there is an element of optimism and joie de vivre. Many millionaires know that if things go wrong, it is possible to find the bright side, learn from mistakes, and move on. Additionally, many millionaires know how to enjoy life as well. Many successful and happy millionaires understand that there is more to life than just amassing wealth; sometimes you need to spend time with your family and friends, eat good food and relax a little. However, the ability to find a silver lining, and to have the persistence to try again, is one of the defining traits of a millionaire.

5. Willing to Get Their Hands Dirty

Sometimes, it takes a little elbow grease to get there. Or, if you are running a business, it might take some late nights. Millionaires are willing to work hard and do things for themselves when they need to. Millionaires are also willing to do what it takes, even if it means taking on an unpleasant job. A millionaire also knows that this includes taking responsibility for his or her financial destiny, refusing to blame others for misfortunes and finding ways to make sure income streams are diverse.

Is Becoming Wealthy Really that Simple?

Earn money, spend less than you earn, save, invest, repeat the process. Embrace the Millionaire Mindset. After that, it's just a matter of time. Even if it takes years or decades, the process really is that simple. Of course, it may not seem as easy as I laid it out here, but it really is. Remember, this is not an overnight get rich quick scheme. It takes time, planning, and a little luck along the way.

HOW TO MANAGE YOUR FINANCES

People often believe that in order to achieve financial freedom it is all about making more and more money. Once you have made some mysterious number instantly all will be better and you will; have all you ever wanted and everything will be right with the world. Unfortunately just making more money isn't enough to truly become financial freedom. Financial freedom is about more than income, it is about changing how you think about money and more importantly, how you manage your money.

I am a firm believe that it is important that we look and at understand more than just how to make money. We have to know how to manage that money in order to be successful. The effective money management system that works for me and has worked for thousands of others is called the jar system, and it is a simple tool to implement. What you need are six jars (or even easier, one checking account and 5 savings accounts at the same bank). Once these 6 accounts have been set up you will divide your income into these six categories every time new money comes in, and you will only use these monies in the manner the account allows.

1: Necessities (50% of income)

You will take 50% of all of your income and place it into this account. This account covers exactly what it says, your necessities. This would covers such expenses as rent/mortgage, car payments, insurance, food, etc. These are the monthly expenses you have to pay.

I recognize that currently you may have necessary expenses that exceed 50% of your income on a monthly basis. This is ok, the idea is to eventually get down to the 50% amount and keep it at that way. In order to get down to the 50% you have two choices, to make more income or to simplify.

Often simplifying is the most overlooked and easiest answer. Look at your monthly expenses and look for things that you consider needed but really is not. Some of the best examples are cable (do you NEED cable or do you just LIKE tv), eating out (do you eat out often and can you save money by cooking at home more? This can both save money and improve home life), etc. Be honest with yourself and look for those expenses that you like but you do not HAVE to have.

2: Financial Freedom (20% of income)

This is the single most important account, and often can be the toughest account to create and maintain. This is 20% of your income and you can never touch or spend this money. This is the money you are putting aside for your long term financial freedom. This is the money that can only be used to create more income, but the key here is that it can only be used to create PASSIVE income. Eventually you want to replace all of your income with passive income, income that comes

100

in whether you work or not. If you do not understand what passive income is, then just leave this money in this account and do NOT touch it until you understand passive income. This money is investment in your long term financial freedom, so guard it very carefully.

3: Education (10% of income)

This is the second most important account next to your financial freedom account. If you are not learning you are dying, so keep growing and becoming better by investing in your education. Once we start working hard on education we get addicted to the learning and growth and want to do more and more and more of it. This is why this account exists, it honors and funds your learning, but also helps to give you guidance on how much you are allowed to use for your growth.

So make sure you are getting consistent education, just make cure you have it under control when you are doing it. This can be doing personal development courses, or learning new ways to invest money, to make your financial freedom account grow, etc. These courses should be anything that helps you become a better person and helps to move your towards financial freedom.

4: Long Term Savings for Spending (10% of your income)

Sometimes we have a larger priced item that we want to get, like a new flat screen tv, a new car, etc. Instead of just running out, buying it with a credit card, and spending a lot of time paying off these larger ticket items, this account exists. You put money into this account and let it grow over time until you can pay for that larger ticket item. If you want to take the family to Disney for a week, you need to figure out how much that will cost and then put the money aside for this into the account. Once you have enough money in this account to cover the full cost of the trip, then you can go on the trip. Often these large ticket items are what kill our budget and this account helps us learn to be more responsible.

5: Play (10% of your income)

I kept this account for last because I believe it is be the most important one to get good at and also know it is the most counter intuitive account. This account is 10% of your income and you MUST blow this money every month on something you would not spend money on usually. This is the money to spoil yourself and do the thing you think you cannot do because you "cannot afford it". This is the account to be used on the limo to and from the airport, or on the fancy dinner at the best restaurant in town, or ordering a bottle of wine without looking at the prices etc. This is the account to train you to think and act like a millionaire. I know it seems counter intuitive to blow 10% of your money on things that may seem frivolous, but trust me, if you get this part of the jar system down, it will change your life.

I have known people who have signed recording contracts because they spent their play jar on a first class ticket which led to them sitting next to a producer, etc. This is common place for people who use their play jar to dine out at a fine restaurant and get seated next to a major player in their city who was looking to fund the exact project they were looking for funding on. Honor the power of this jar and it will pay you back many fold.

Now I understand that not everyone is in the place to do this program exactly as outlined here. You finances may require you to spend 85% of your income on necessities right now. That is fine, make sure you are getting your bills paid, but also look for ways to simplify to get that percentage down. Implementing this simple money management system you will start to feel financially free.

STEPS TO SAFE INVESTING IN RETIREMENT

Investing in retirement can be daunting and even scary, but following certain principles will allow you to manage your retirement account profitably.

You can actually simplify the management of your retirement without giving up control by self-managing your retirement account if you follow certain key principles. These principles don't require a lot of time, because your time is precious, but do require the decision that you want your future to be how you define it and not how someone else sees you.

The 5 key Steps or Principles are:

Recognize your retirement future

Define how to manage your retirement

Confirm your time

Establish a method

Keep your focus

Recognize your retirement future

Sure, you may have a 401k or an IRA but that doesn't mean you really, truly have recognized its importance to your future. The fact that a retirement account exists is only part of the recognition. The other part is knowing or planning what you want from your account. This means thinking about how much money you will need in the future because even with social security you will need more, lots more to live the way you do now or better, to travel, to go to the movies or buy new shoes.

Define how to Manage your Retirement Account

You have choices on how to manage your retirement account:

1. Let your employer's administrator do it

2. Hire a professional (if your account is big enough) & pay fees

3. Take control yourself

Confirm your time:

No time whatsoever - then either #1 or #2 above

30 minutes or 1 hour a week - then #3 - you can take control yourself

No time limit - again, #3 - you can take control yourself

Establish a method

To self-manage your retirement portfolio you will need investment software. There are many types:

Brokers websites - many offer the ability to screen based on different criteria such as return or size.

Charting software that can give you buy-sell signals on funds, stocks or ETFs that you pick -

presuming you understand how to read or configure the various chart types.

Comprehensive software that lets you pick a method of analysis and then gives recommendations and charts for what to buy from a group or universe of funds, ETS or stocks, plus when to sell based upon different criteria. This type software usually has an optimization or back test feature to find the best buy-sell rules that meet your goals and desires. Dynamic Investor Pro fits this category and requires as little as 30 minutes a week.

Keep your focus

Once you are on your path to taking control of your retirement future it is essential to keep your focus and develop a habit of checking your portfolio. This doesn't mean you have to look at every day or become obsessed with it. All you need, with the right investment software, is 30 minutes a week or even every month.

Again the key is to establish a habit, just like anything else you do on a regular basis. Think of it as baking a cake - as long as you keep the cupboard & refrigerator stocked with ingredients by looking them over every week before you go shopping, you will be prepared.

BECOMING A MILLIONAIRE METHOD

A great many people aspire to become a millionaire, but not so many people are pushing themselves hard enough to reach that particular goal. In a world where being a billionaire is now the new target for the rich, becoming a millionaire is a real possibility for many an average Joe, and it mostly comes down to good management, sensible thinking and occasional calculated risks.

Preparing for Success

Set yourself concrete goals. Good preparation is an absolute necessity when it comes to endeavors as big as becoming a millionaire. And it all starts with giving yourself concrete, measurable goals that you can keep your eyes on.

Perhaps you want to reach millionaire status by a certain age, like 30.

Or perhaps your first goal is just to be out of debt within two years.

Break bigger goals into more actionable smaller goals. For example, if one of your goals is to have a growing business in a year, start with the goal of fleshing out a business model within the first month.

Get a good education. Although there are a number of examples of millionaires and billionaires who never completed college, statistics show a link between education and wealth. The higher your level of education, the more opportunities are unlocked for you, and the higher the chance that you will become a millionaire.

Take care of your health. Making money and making good decisions that create more money in your life require that you are in good shape. Keep fit, eat well, and take good care of your body. It is your health that will provide you with the energy and resources needed to keep going on the commitment to becoming a millionaire.

Be tenacious. Success requires an ability to keep getting up after failures. There will be plenty of failures as you try to find the best ways to make a million or more. This isn't about the safety net of an average salary and the boss's orders being met each day. To become a millionaire, you have to be prepared to make decisions that won't always succeed but if the risks aren't taken, then the potential for success won't be realized either.

Check your self-confidence. If it's low, now is the time to build it up. High self-esteem and good self-confidence are essential traits to help you on your way. However, don't let this delay you. You can fake it until you make it and the more you practice being confident, the sooner it becomes a part of who you are.

Read the advice of those who've made it. Benefitting from the wisdom of the successful can never hurt, but be careful not to get caught up in the planning and preparing stage. The most important step is taking action. However, do spend some time reading other millionaires' advice.

Find a mentor who has walked the walk and seek advice. Surround yourself with already-made millionaires. They can be found in several places, there's even a private online club where you can have a millionaire mentor personally show you how to make money in many areas online.

Managing Your Money

Stop spending and be thrifty. This is a key element of becoming a millionaire. Either you have the money in savings or you're spending it on things. You can't have both if you're aiming to become a millionaire. Most millionaires (a net worth of $1 million to $10 million) are living a very frugal and cost-effective life, without hyper-expenditure.

This includes:

Live beneath your means. A good rule of thumb for your living situation is to spend no more than one third of your monthly salary on rent.

Buy quality clothing but don't pay ridiculous prices. A suit under $400 will do you just fine.

Wear inexpensive watches, jewelry, and accessories.

Don't collect things.

Drive a reliable but affordable car of an ordinary brand.

Avoid prestige and luxury brands.

Stop comparing yourself to others and trying to keep up with them through spending.

Familiarize yourself with savings. If you're used to maxing out the credit card and not saving much, you're going to find it hard to become a millionaire at any stage in your lifetime. Begin by opening a savings account purely for keeping aside money and add to it regularly. This should be different from your every day savings account that you use to draw bill payments from and it should preferably be one that has a higher interest rate than your usual savings account options.

Having a savings account is one of the many ways where you can set your money up to work for you. Your initial deposit of money grows whether you make additional deposits by interest. Learn the different types of accounts, including accounts like IRAs.

Saving money requires good self-discipline. Spend time working on any bad habits that take away from your self-discipline. Focus on what you can accomplish by saving rather than hoarding stuff or showing off to others through conspicuous consumption.

Invest in stocks. If you're gung-ho for individual stocks, buy stocks of the companies whose products and services you use or purchase. One of the best ways to invest in individual stocks is through an investment club; you may want to consider forming one with your friends. However, whatever way you choose to buy stocks, get really sound and good financial advice first. Do your due diligence on that financial advisor - check their reputation and record of accomplishment first.

Buy mutual funds. Mutual funds are an investment of other investments. When you own a mutual fund, you own the securities (stocks, bonds, cash) within the mutual. With mutual funds, you are pooling your money with other investors and diversifying your investment.

Getting Into Business

Look at what people need, not necessarily at what you want when deciding on a business. There will always be things people need and they need them to be done well. Things like garbage disposal, energy creation, providing products to the health and dying industries, etc. In addition, the certainty of customers should not be overlooked lightly. Choose a business that provides what people really need and be prepared to put in the effort to make your products and services either the best, the most price efficient or unique.

Have a frugal start up. There is much talk about "looking the part". There isn't much point looking the part if it cost an arm and a leg to get it and you lack clients to pay for it. Get yourself a fabulous suit that is worn every day and makes you feel confident and ready to meet people but be very careful with your office fit-out and other business elements.

Here are some ideas to help you initially:

Consider renting offices that someone else furnishes, cleans and that get shared around.

Spend only the time needed in them, to cut costs.

If you do have your own offices, rent furniture or buy it cheap at auction.

Lease anything that needs to be constantly updated, computers being number one in this group.

Keep staff expenses under strict control from the beginning.

Fly economy. Or use Skype and other online forms of virtual conferencing and avoid flying at all.

Be eco-aware and turn off unused items all the time. Save the planet and your bottom line.

Monitor cashflow with an eagle eye in your start up business. This is one time in life where obsession is a good quality. Every cent counts and if it's not in your savings or being churned back into your business, it's in someone else's pocket.

Don't neglect the viability of your business. Always pay attention to what isn't working and remedy it at the earliest possible opportunity.

Don't neglect the mundane but essential parts of running a business, like timesheets, tax, petty cash, invoicing, etc. Do them with clockwork regularity or employ someone who is capable to deal with these things.

Deal with bad debt as soon as it rears its head. It isn't going away, so the earlier you face it, the better.

Find your business sweet spot. There are only three pieces to this. First, know your strengths that are unique to you, or at least where you can add unique value. Then find a market, a group of people, who want what you have to offer. Finally, you have to make sure those people will pay money for what you have to offer.

Define your brand. A brand is nothing more than a belief system that people have about you and your business. People will want to do business with somebody or some company they believe will solve a specific problem they have. You must be seen as the solution to that problem.

Create your business model. Your business model must be either high fidelity or high convenience. If it's high fidelity you will have fewer customers who will pay a lot. You need 100 customers at $10,000 each to make $1 million. If it's high convenience you will have many customers paying you small amounts. You need 100,000 customers paying you $10 each to make $1 million.

Decide on your exit strategy. The simplest way to make $1 million is to create a business, an asset that you can sell. People will often pay two times the annual earnings for a business. That means a $500,000 a year business can be sold for $1 million. That breaks down to having a business that makes roughly $40,000 per month.

Make more profits from existing customers. The fastest way to increase your income is to sell more products and services to your existing customers. Find ways to add even more value, and offer the products and services to your existing customer base.

Build systems and scale up. This a key entire secret to a massively accelerating your income growth. If you create a product that sells for $100, and you know that $50 spent on advertising consistently produces one sale, you have a winning model, as long as you've picked a large market. Scale up.

Hire great people. One of the biggest way to go from a $60,000 a year income to a multi-million dollar business is by hiring great people. This is why all the large corporations focus on team-building and leadership. It is the only way to have a great team is to be a great leader

INCONCLUSION

Millionaire income level is developed all the same way. To become a millionaire, it is really a very simple journey that you can begin on as soon as you decide to. Every day I start out reviewing my goals and plan to develop financial security. Even during these troubled economic conditions there are ways of mastering wealth creation. You just need to be prepared for the opportunities to generate wealth when they present themselves

Get control of your finances. Nothing could be more important than this step, no matter where you are in your plan to create more wealth, you need to evaluate your current financial situation, begin to reduce any frivolous debt, control outgoing expenditures, and regain control of your finances. Yes the old saying is true today as it was in days past, "it takes money to make money." get control of your finances, establish an operating budget, stick to it everyday and invest.

Made in the USA
Monee, IL
12 February 2022

91180767R00073